Key Facts™ on Argentina

Essential Information on Argentina

By Patrick W. Nee

The Internationalist ®
www.internationalist.com

The Internationalist®

International Business, Investment, and Travel

Published by:

The Internationalist Publishing Company

96 Walter Street/ Suite 200

Boston, MA 02131, USA

Tel: 617-354-7722

www.internationalist.com

PN@internationalist.com

Copyright © 2013 by PWN

The Internationalist is a Registered Trademark. "Key Facts" and "The Internationalist Business Guides" are Trademarks of The Internationalist Publishing Company.

All Rights are reserved under International, Pan-American, and Pan-Asian Conventions. No part of this book may be reproduced in any form without the written permission of the publisher. All rights vigorously enforced

Table of Contents

Chapter 1: Background…5

Chapter 2: Geography…6

Chapter 3: People & Society…11

Chapter 4: Government…19

Chapter 5: Economy…26

Chapter 6: Energy…36

Chapter 7: Communications…41

Chapter 8: Transportation…43

Chapter 9: Military…46

Chapter 10: Transnational Issues…48

Chapter 1: Background

In 1816, the United Provinces of the Rio Plata declared their independence from Spain. After Bolivia, Paraguay, and Uruguay went their separate ways, the area that remained became Argentina. The country's population and culture were heavily shaped by immigrants from throughout Europe, with Italy and Spain providing the largest percentage of newcomers from 1860 to 1930. Up until about the mid-20th century, much of Argentina's history was dominated by periods of internal political conflict between Federalists and Unitarians and between civilian and military factions. After World War II, an era of Peronist populism and direct and indirect military interference in subsequent governments was followed by a military junta that took power in 1976. Democracy returned in 1983 after a failed bid to seize the Falkland Islands (Islas Malvinas) by force, and has persisted despite numerous challenges, the most formidable of which was a severe economic crisis in 2001-02 that led to violent public protests and the successive resignations of several presidents

Chapter 2: Geography

Location:
>Southern South America, bordering the South Atlantic Ocean, between Chile and Uruguay

Geographic Coordinates:
>34 00 S, 64 00 W

Map References:
>South America

Area:
>**total:** 2,780,400 sq km
>**country comparison to the world:** 8
>**land:** 2,736,690 sq km
>**water:** 43,710 sq km

Area-Comparative:
>Slightly less than three-tenths the size of the US

Land Boundaries:
>**total:** 9,861 km
>**border countries:** Bolivia 832 km, Brazil 1,261 km, Chile 5,308 km, Paraguay 1,880 km, Uruguay 580 km

Coastline:
>4,989 km

Maritime Claims:
>**territorial sea:** 12 nm
>**contiguous zone:** 24 nm
>**exclusive economic zone:** 200 nm

continental shelf: 200 nm or to the edge of the continental margin

Climate:
Mostly temperate; arid in southeast; subantarctic in southwest

Terrain:
Rich plains of the Pampas in northern half, flat to rolling plateau of Patagonia in south, rugged Andes along western border

Elevation Extremes:
Lowest point: Laguna del Carbon -105 m (located between Puerto San Julian and Comandante Luis Piedra Buena in the province of Santa Cruz)
Highest point: Cerro Aconcagua 6,960 m (located in the northwestern corner of the province of Mendoza)

Natural Resources:
Fertile plains of the pampas, lead, zinc, tin, copper, iron ore, manganese, petroleum, uranium

Land Use
Arable land: 10.03%
Permanent crops: 0.36%
Other: 89.61% (2005)

Irrigated Land:
15,500 sq km (2003)

Total Renewable Water Resources:
814 cu km (2000)

Freshwater Withdrawal—(Domestic/Industrial/Agricultural):
>total: 29.19 cu km/yr (17%/9%/74%)
>
>per capita: 753 cu m/yr (2000)

Natural Hazards:
>San Miguel de Tucuman and Mendoza areas in the Andes subject to earthquakes; pamperos are violent windstorms that can strike the pampas and northeast; heavy flooding in some areas.
>
>Volcanism: volcanic activity in the Andes Mountains along the Chilean border; Copahue (elev. 2,997 m) last erupted in 2000; other historically active volcanoes include Llullaillaco, Maipo, Planchon-Peteroa, San Jose, Tromen, Tupungatito, and Viedma.

Environment—Current Issues:
>Environmental problems (urban and rural) typical of an industrializing economy such as deforestation, soil degradation, desertification, air pollution, and water pollution note: Argentina is a world leader in setting voluntary greenhouse gas targets.

Environment—International Agreements:
>Party to: Antarctic-Environmental Protocol, Antarctic-Marine Living Resources, Antarctic Seals, Antarctic Treaty, Biodiversity, Climate Change, Climate Change-Kyoto Protocol, Desertification, Endangered Species, Environmental Modification, Hazardous Wastes, Law of the

Sea, Marine Dumping, Ozone Layer Protection, Ship Pollution, Wetlands, Whaling

Signed, but not ratified: Marine Life Conservation

Geography—Note:

Second-largest country in South America (after Brazil); strategic location relative to sea lanes between the South Atlantic and the South Pacific Oceans (Strait of Magellan, Beagle Channel, Drake Passage); diverse geophysical landscapes range from tropical climates in the north to tundra in the far south; Cerro Aconcagua is the Western Hemisphere's tallest mountain, while Laguna del Carbon is the lowest point in the Western Hemisphere

Chapter 3: People and Society

Nationality:

Noun: Argentine(s)

Adjective: Argentine

Ethnic Groups

White (mostly Spanish and Italian) 97%, mestizo (mixed white and Amerindian ancestry), Amerindian, or other non-white groups 3%

Languages:

Spanish (official), Italian, English, German, French, indigenous (Mapudungun, Quechua)

Religions:

Nominally Roman Catholic 92% (less than 20% practicing), Protestant 2%, Jewish 2%, other 4%

Demographic Profile:

Argentina's population continues to grow but at a slower rate because of its steadily declining birth rate. Argentina's fertility decline began earlier than in the rest of Latin America, occurring most rapidly between the early 20th century and the 1950s and then becoming more gradual. Life expectancy has been improving, most notably among the young and the poor. While the population under age 15 is shrinking, the youth cohort - ages 15 - 24 - is the largest in Argentina's history and will continue to bolster the working-age population. If this large working-age population is well-educated and gainfully employed, Argentina is likely to experience an economic boost and possibly higher per capita savings and investment. Although literacy and primary school enrollment are nearly universal, grade repetition is problematic and secondary school completion is low. Both of these issues vary widely by region and socioeconomic group.

Argentina has been primarily a country of immigration for most of its history, welcoming European immigrants after its independence in the 19th century and attracting especially large numbers from Spain and Italy. European immigration diminished in the 1950s, when Argentina's military dictatorships tightened immigration rules and European economies rebounded. Regional migration, however, continued to supply low-skilled workers and today it accounts for three-quarters of Argentina's immigrant population. The first waves of highly skilled Argentine emigrant workers headed mainly to the United States and Spain in the 1960s and 1970s. The ongoing European economic crisis is driving the return migration of some Argentinean and other Latin American nationals, as well as the immigration of Europeans to South America, where Argentina is a key recipient.

Population:

42,192,494 (July 2012 est.)

Country comparison to the world: 32

Age Structure:

0-14 years: 25.2% (male 5,450,679/female 5,200,704)

15-24 years: 15.9% (male 3,426,818/female 3,292,391)

25-54 years: 38.7% (male 8,130,169/female 8,187,515)

55-64 years: 9% (male 1,844,010/female 1,961,042)

65 years and over: 11.1% (male 1,940,810/female 2,758,356) (2012 est.)

Median Age:

total: 30.7 years

male: 29.7 years

female: 31.8 years (2012 est.)

Population Growth Rate:

0.997% (2012 est.)

Country comparison to the world: 116

Birth Rate:

17.34 births/1,000 population (2012 est.)

Country comparison to the world: 113

Death Rate:

7.36 deaths/1,000 population (July 2012 est.)

Country comparison to the world: 118

Net Migration Rate:

0 migrant(s)/1,000 population (2012 est.)

Country comparison to the world: 74

Urbanization:

Urban population: 92% of total population (2010)

Rate of urbanization: 1.1% annual rate of change (2010-15 est.)

Major Cities—Population:

BUENOS AIRES (capital) 12.988 million;

Cordoba 1.493 million;

Rosario 1.231 million;

Mendoza 917,000;

San Miguel de Tucuman 831,000 (2009)

Sex Ratio:

At birth: 1.05 male(s)/female

Under 15 years: 1.05 male(s)/female

15-64 years: 1 male(s)/female

65 years and over: 0.7 male(s)/female

Total population: 0.97 male(s)/female (2011 est.)

Maternal Mortality Rate

77 deaths/100,000 live births (2010)

Country comparison to the world: 84

Infant Mortality Rate:

Total: 10.52 deaths/1,000 live births

Country comparison to the world: 143

Male: 11.76 deaths/1,000 live births

Female: 9.22 deaths/1,000 live births (2012 est.)

Life Expectancy at Birth:

Total population: 77.14 years

Country comparison to the world: 69

Male: 73.9 years

Female: 80.54 years (2012 est.)

Health Expenditures

9.5% of GDP (2009)

Country comparison to the world: 37

Physicians Density:

3.155 physicians/1,000 population (2004)

Hospital Bed Density:

4 beds/1,000 population (2005)

Sanitation Facility Access:

Improved:

Urban: 91% of population

Rural: 77% of population

Total: 90% of population

Unimproved:

Urban: 9% of population

Rural: 23% of population

Total: 10% of population

HIV/AIDS—Adult Prevalence Rate:

0.5% (2009 est.)

Country comparison to the world: 66

HIV/AIDS—People Living with HIV/AIDS

110,000 (2009 est.)

Country comparison to the world: 39

HIV/AIDS—Deaths:

2,900 (2009 est.)

Country comparison to the world: 46

Major Infectious Diseases:

Degree of risk: intermediate

Food or waterborne diseases: bacterial diarrhea, hepatitis A

Water contact disease: leptospirosis (2009)

Children Under the Age of 5 Years Underweight:

2.3% (2005)

Country comparison to the world: 106

Education Expenditures:

4.9% of GDP (2007)

Country comparison to the world: 63

Literacy:

Definition: age 15 and over can read and write

Total population: 97.2%

Male: 97.2%

Female: 97.2% (2001 census)

School Life Expectancy (Primary to Tertiary Education):

Total: 16 years

Male: 15 years

Female: 17 years (2007)

Unemployment, Youth Ages 15-24:

Total: 21.2%

Country comparison to the world: 50

Male: 18.8%

Female: 24.7% (2009)

Chapter 4: Government

Country Name:

Conventional long form: Argentine Republic

Conventional short form: Argentina

Local long form: Republica Argentina

Local short form: Argentina

Government Type:

Republic

Capital:

Name: Buenos Aires

Geographic coordinates: 34 35 S, 58 40 W

Time difference: UTC-3 (2 hours ahead of Washington, DC during Standard Time)

Daylight saving time: none scheduled for 2011

Administrative Divisions:

23 provinces (provincias, singular - provincia) and 1 autonomous city*; Buenos Aires, Catamarca, Chaco, Chubut, Ciudad Autonoma de Buenos Aires*, Cordoba, Corrientes, Entre Rios, Formosa, Jujuy, La Pampa, La Rioja, Mendoza, Misiones, Neuquen, Rio Negro, Salta, San Juan, San Luis, Santa Cruz, Santa Fe, Santiago del Estero, Tierra del Fuego - Antartida e Islas del Atlantico Sur (Tierra del Fuego), Tucuman

Note: the US does not recognize any claims to Antarctica

Independence:

9 July 1816 (from Spain)

National Holiday:
Revolution Day, 25 May (1810)

Constitution:
1 May 1853; amended many times starting in 1860

Legal System:
Civil law system based on West European legal systems; note—efforts at civil code reform begun in the mid-1980s has stagnated

International Law Organization Participation:
Has not submitted an ICJ jurisdiction declaration; accepts ICCt jurisdiction

Suffrage:
18-70 years of age; universal and compulsory; 16-17 years of age - optional

Executive Branch:
- Chief of State: President Cristina FERNANDEZ DE KIRCHNER (since 10 December 2007)
- Vice President Amado BOUDOU (since 10 December 2011); note - the president is both the chief of state and head of government
- Head of Government: President Cristina FERNANDEZ DE KIRCHNER (since 10 December 2007)
- Vice President Amado BOUDOU (since 10 December 2011)
- Cabinet: Cabinet appointed by the president

- (For more information visit the World Leaders website)
- Elections: president and vice president elected on the same ticket by popular vote for four-year terms (eligible for a second term); election last held on 23 October 2011 (next election to be held in October 2015)
- Election results: Cristina FERNANDEZ DE KIRCHNER reelected president; percent of vote - Cristina FERNANDEZ DE KIRCHNER 54%, Hermes BINNER 16.9%, Ricardo ALFONSIN 11.1%, Alberto Rodriguez SAA 8%, Eduardo DUHALDE 5.9%, other 4.1%

Legislative Branch:

- Bicameral National Congress or Congreso Nacional consists of the Senate (72 seats; members are elected by direct vote; presently one-third of the members elected every two years to serve six-year terms) and the Chamber of Deputies (257 seats; members are elected by direct vote; one-half of the members elected every two years to serve four-year terms)
- Elections: Senate - last held on 23 October 2011 (next to be held in 2013); Chamber of Deputies - last held on 23 October 2011 (next to be held in 2013)
- Election results: Senate - percent of vote by bloc or party - NA; seats by bloc or party - FpV 38, UCR 17,

PJ Disidente 10, FAP 4, other 3; Chamber of Deputies - percent of vote by bloc or party - NA; seats by bloc or party - FpV 134, UCR 41, PJ Disidente 28, FAP 22, PRO 11, CC 7, other 14; note - as of 1 January 2013, the composition of the entire legislature is as follows: Senate - seats by bloc or party - FpV 32, UCR 14, PJ Disidente 9, minor parties allied with the FpV 6, FAP 4, other 7; Chamber of Deputies - percent of vote by bloc or party - NA; seats by bloc or party - FpV 116, UCR 40, PJ Disidente 22, FAP 22, minor parties allied with the FpV 20, PRO 11, CC 6, other 20

Judicial Branch:

- Supreme Court or Corte Suprema (the Supreme Court judges are appointed by the president with approval of the Senate)
- Note: the Supreme Court has seven judges; the Argentine Congress in 2006 passed a bill to gradually reduce the number of Supreme Court judges to five

Political Parties and Leaders:

Broad Progressive Front or FAP [Hermes BINNER]; Civic Coalition or CC (a broad coalition loosely affiliated with Elisa CARRIO); Dissident Peronists (PJ Disidente) or Federal Peronism (a sector of the Justicialist Party opposed to the Kirchners); Front for Victory or FpV (a broad coalition, including elements of the PJ, UCR, and numerous provincial parties) [Cristina FERNANDEZ DE KIRCHNER]; Peronist (or Justicialist) Party or PJ [vacant]; Radical Civic Union or UCR [Mario BARLETTA]; Republican Proposal or PRO [Mauricio MACRI]; Socialist Party or PS [Ruben GIUSTINIANI]; numerous provincial parties

Political Pressure Groups and Leaders:

Argentine Association of Pharmaceutical Labs (CILFA); Argentine Industrial Union (manufacturers' association); Argentine Rural Confederation or CRA (small to medium landowners' association); Argentine Rural Society (large landowners' association); Central of Argentine Workers or CTA (a union for employed and unemployed workers); General Confederation of Labor or CGT (Peronist-leaning umbrella labor organization); White and Blue CGT (dissident CGT labor confederation); Roman Catholic Church
other: business organizations; Peronist-dominated labor movement; Piquetero groups (popular protest organizations that can be either pro or anti-government); students

International Organization Participation:

AfDB (nonregional member), Australia Group, BCIE, BIS, CAN (associate), CD, CELAC, FAO, FATF, G-15, G-20, G-24, G-77, IADB, IAEA, IBRD, ICAO, ICC (national committees), ICRM, IDA, IFAD, IFC, IFRCS, IHO, ILO, IMF, IMO, IMSO, Interpol, IOC, IOM, IPU, ISO, ITSO, ITU, ITUC (NGOs), LAES, LAIA, Mercosur, MIGA, MINURSO, MINUSTAH, NAM (observer), NSG, OAS, OPANAL,

OPCW, Paris Club (associate), PCA, SICA (observer), UN, UNASUR, UNCTAD, UNESCO, UNFICYP, UNHCR, UNIDO, Union Latina (observer), UNTSO, UNWTO, UPU, WCO, WFTU (NGOs), WHO, WIPO, WMO, WTO, ZC

Diplomatic Representation in the US:

Chief of Mission: Ambassador Jorge Martin Arturo ARGUELLO

Chancery: 1600 New Hampshire Avenue NW, Washington, DC 20009

Telephone: [1] (202) 238-6400

FAX: [1] (202) 332-3171

Consulate(s) General: Atlanta, Chicago, Houston, Los Angeles, Miami, New York

Diplomatic Representation from the US:

Chief of Mission: Ambassador Vilma MARTINEZ

Embassy: Avenida Colombia 4300, C1425GMN Buenos Aires

Mailing address: international mail: use embassy street address; APO address: US Embassy Buenos Aires, Unit 4334, APO AA 34034

Telephone: [54] (11) 5777-4533

FAX: [54] (11) 5777-4240

Flag Description:

Three equal horizontal bands of light blue (top), white, and light blue; centered in the white band is a radiant yellow sun with a human face known as the Sun of May; the colors represent the clear skies and snow of the Andes; the sun symbol commemorates the appearance of the sun through cloudy skies on 25 May 1810 during the first mass demonstration in favor of independence; the sun features are those of Inti, the Inca god of the sun

National Symbol(s):

Sun of May (a sun-with-face symbol)

National Anthem:

Name: "Himno Nacional Argentino" (Argentine National Anthem)

Lyrics/music: Vicente LOPEZ y PLANES/Jose Blas PARERA

Note: adopted 1813; Vicente LOPEZ was inspired to write the anthem after watching a play about the 1810 May Revolution against Spain

Chapter 5: Economy:

Economy—Overview:

Argentina benefits from rich natural resources, a highly literate population, an export-oriented agricultural sector, and a diversified industrial base. Although one of the world's wealthiest countries 100 years ago, Argentina suffered during most of the 20th century from recurring economic crises, persistent fiscal and current account deficits, high inflation, mounting external debt, and capital flight. A severe depression, growing public and external indebtedness, and an unprecedented bank run culminated in 2001 in the most serious economic, social, and political crisis in the country's turbulent history. Interim President Adolfo RODRIGUEZ SAA declared a default - the largest in history - on the government's foreign debt in December of that year, and abruptly resigned only a few days after taking office. His successor, Eduardo DUHALDE, announced an end to the peso's decade-long 1-to-1 peg to the US dollar in early 2002. The economy bottomed out that year, with real GDP 18% smaller than in 1998 and almost 60% of Argentines under the poverty line. Real GDP rebounded to grow by an average 8.5% annually over the subsequent six years, taking advantage of previously idled industrial capacity and labor, an audacious debt restructuring and reduced debt burden, excellent international financial conditions, and expansionary monetary and fiscal policies. Inflation also increased, however, during the administration of President Nestor KIRCHNER, which responded with price restraints on businesses, as well as export taxes and restraints, and beginning in 2007, with understating inflation data. Cristina FERNANDEZ DE KIRCHNER succeeded her husband as President in late 2007, and the rapid economic growth of previous years began to slow sharply the following year as government policies held back exports and the world economy fell into recession. The economy in 2010 rebounded strongly from the 2009 recession, but has slowed since late 2011 even as the government continued to rely on expansionary fiscal and monetary policies, which have kept inflation in the double digits.

GDP (Purchasing Power Parity):

$746.9 billion (2012 est.)

Country comparison to the world: 22

$728.1 billion (2011 est.)

$668.8 billion (2010 est.)

Note: data are in 2012 US dollars

GDP (Official Exchange Rate)

$474.8 billion (2012 est.)

GDP—Real Growth Rate:

2.6% (2012 est.)

Country comparison to the world: 124

8.9% (2011 est.)

9.2% (2010 est.)

GDP per Capita (PPP):

$18,200 (2012 est.)

Country comparison to the world: 67

$17,900 (2011 est.)

$16,700 (2010 est.)

Note: data are in 2012 US dollars

GDP—Composition by Sector:

Agriculture: 10.3%

Industry: 30.6%

Services: 59.1% (2012 est.)

Labor Force:

17.07 million

Country comparison to the world: 36

Note: urban areas only (2012 est.)

Labor Force—By Occupation:

Agriculture: 5%

Industry: 23%

Services: 72% (2009 est.)

Unemployment Rate:

7.2% (2012 est.)

Country comparison to the world: 80

7.2% (2011 est.)

Population Below the Poverty Line:

30%

Note: data are based on private estimates (2010)

Household Income or Consumption by Percentage Share:
    Lowest 10%: 1.5%
    Highest 10%: 32.3% (2010 est.)

Distribution of Family Income—Gini Index:
    45.8 (2009)
    Country comparison to the world: 35

Investment (Gross Fixed):
    19.2% of GDP (2012 est.)
    Country comparison to the world: 110

Budget:
    Revenues: $117.5 billion
    Expenditures: $132.8 billion (2012 est.)

Taxes and Other Revenues:
    24.7% of GDP (2012 est.)
    Country comparison to the world: 128

Budget Surplus (+) or Deficit (-):
    -3.2% of GDP (2012 est.)
    Country comparison to the world: 112

Public Debt:
    41.6% of GDP (2012 est.)
    Country comparison to the world: 85
    41.7% of GDP (2011 est.)

Inflation Rate (Consumer Prices):
    25% (2012 est.)
    Country comparison to the world: 220
    21% (2011 est.)

Note: data are derived from private estimates

Commercial Bank Prime Lending Rate:
> 14.4% (31 December 2012 est.)
>
> Country comparison to the world: 57
>
> 14.09% (31 December 2011 est.)

Stock of Narrow Money:
> $60.66 billion (31 December 2012 est.)
>
> Country comparison to the world: 45
>
> $50.25 billion (31 December 2011 est.)

Stock of Broad Money:
> $148.6 billion (31 December 2012 est.)
>
> Country comparison to the world: 50
>
> $123.7 billion (31 December 2011 est.)

Stock of Domestic Credit:
> $158.7 billion (31 December 2012 est.)
>
> Country comparison to the world: 45
>
> $132.2 billion (31 December 2011 est.)

Market Value of Publicly Traded Shares:
> $43.58 billion (31 December 2011)
>
> Country comparison to the world: 50
>
> $63.91 billion (31 December 2010)
>
> $48.93 billion (31 December 2009)

Agriculture—Products:
> Sunflower seeds, lemons, soybeans, grapes, corn, tobacco, peanuts, tea, wheat; livestock

Industrial Production Growth Rate:

6.5%

Country comparison to the world: 49

Note: based on private estimates (2011 est.)

Current Account Balance:

$1.433 billion (2012 est.)

Country comparison to the world: 40

-$6 million (2011 est.)

Exports:

$85.36 billion (2012 est.)

Country comparison to the world: 45

$84.32 billion (2011 est.)

Exports—Commodities:

Soybeans and derivatives, petroleum and gas, vehicles, corn, wheat

Exports—Partners:

Brazil 21.6%, China 7.3%, Chile 5.5%, US 5.5% (2011)

Imports:

$67.33 billion (2012 est.)

Country comparison to the world: 45

$70.76 billion (2011 est.)

Imports—Commodities:

Machinery, motor vehicles, petroleum and natural gas, organic chemicals, plastics

Imports—Partners

Brazil 33.2%, US 14.4%, China 12.4%, Germany 4.7% (2011)

Reserves of Foreign Exchange and Gold:

$41.2 billion (31 December 2012 est.)

Country comparison to the world: 44

$46.35 billion (31 December 2011 est.)

Debt—External:

$130.2 billion (31 December 2012 est.)

Country comparison to the world: 36

$136.8 billion (31 December 2011 est.)

Stock of Direct Foreign Investment—At Home:

$100.4 billion (31 December 2012 est.)

Country comparison to the world: 40

$93.93 billion (31 December 2011 est.)

Stock of Direct Foreign Investment—Abroad:

$32.73 billion (31 December 2012 est.)

Country comparison to the world: 40

$31.33 billion (31 December 2011 est.)

Exchange Rates:

Argentine pesos (ARS) per US dollar -

4.569 (2012 est.)

4.1101 (2011 est.)

3.8963 (2010 est.)

3.7101 (2009)

3.1636 (2008)

Fiscal Year:

Calendar year

Chapter 6: Energy

Electricity—Production:

    116 billion kWh (2009 est.)

    Country comparison to the world: 31

Electricity—Consumption:

    104.2 billion kWh (2009 est.)

    Country comparison to the world: 31

Electricity—Exports:

    1.701 billion kWh (2010 est.)

    Country comparison to the world: 50

Electricity—Imports:

    10.3 billion kWh (2010 est.)

    Country comparison to the world: 24

Electricity—Installed Generating Capacity:

    32.07 million kW (2009 est.)

    Country comparison to the world: 27

Electricity—From Fossil Fuels:

    65.4% of total installed capacity (2009 est.)

    Country comparison to the world: 126

Electricity—From Nuclear Fuels:

    3.2% of total installed capacity (2009 est.)

    Country comparison to the world: 26

Electricity—From Hydroelectric Plants:

    28.3% of total installed capacity (2009 est.)

    Country comparison to the world: 81

Electricity—From Other Renewable Sources:

0.1% of total installed capacity (2009 est.)

Country comparison to the world: 97

Crude Oil—Production:

734,000 bbl/day (2011 est.)

Country comparison to the world: 26

Crude Oil—Exports:

93,600 bbl/day (2009 est.)

Country comparison to the world: 38

Crude Oil—Imports:

0 bbl/day (2009 est.)

Country comparison to the world: 155

Crude Oil—Proved Reserves:

2.82 billion bbl (1 January 2013 est.)

Country comparison to the world: 33

Refined Petroleum Products—Production:

604,200 bbl/day (2008 est.)

Country comparison to the world: 30

Refined Petroleum Products—Consumption:

678,100 bbl/day (2011 est.)

Country comparison to the world: 29

Refined Petroleum Products—Exports:

66,700 bbl/day (2008 est.)

Country comparison to the world: 52

Refined Petroleum Products—Imports:

37,260 bbl/day (2008 est.)

Country comparison to the world: 79

Natural Gas—Production:

    40.1 billion cu m (2010 est.)

    Country comparison to the world: 25

Natural Gas—Consumption:

    43.29 billion cu m (2010 est.)

    Country comparison to the world: 23

Natural Gas—Exports:

    420 million cu m (2010 est.)

    Country comparison to the world: 44

Natural Gas—Imports:

    3.61 billion cu m (2010 est.)

    Country comparison to the world: 39

Natural Gas—Proved Reserves:

    378.8 billion cu m (1 January 2012 est.)

    Country comparison to the world: 37

Carbon Dioxide Emissions from Consumption of Energy:

    169.8 million Mt (2010 est.)

    Country comparison to the world: 32

Chapter 7: Communication

Telephones—Main Lines in Use:

    10.14 million (2011)

    Country comparison to the world: 22

Telephones—Mobile Cellular:

    55 million (2011)

    Country comparison to the world: 24

Telephone System:

- General assessment: in 1998 Argentina opened its telecommunications market to competition and foreign investment encouraging the growth of modern telecommunications technology; fiber-optic cable trunk lines are being installed between all major cities; major networks are entirely digital and the availability of telephone service is improving
- Domestic: microwave radio relay, fiber-optic cable, and a domestic satellite system with 40 earth stations serve the trunk network; fixed-line teledensity is increasing gradually and mobile-cellular subscribership is increasing rapidly; broadband Internet services are gaining ground
- International: country code - 54; landing point for the Atlantis-2, UNISUR, South America-1, and South American Crossing/Latin American Nautilus submarine cable systems that provide links to Europe, Africa, South and Central America, and US; satellite

earth stations - 112; 2 international gateways near Buenos Aires (2011)

Broadcast Media:

Government owns a TV station and a radio network; more than 2 dozen TV stations and hundreds of privately-owned radio stations; high rate of cable TV subscription usage (2007)

Internet Country Code:

.ar

Internet Hosts:

11.232 million (2012)

Country comparison to the world: 13

Internet Users:

13.694 million (2009)

Country comparison to the world: 28

Chapter 8: Transportation:

Airports:

    1,149 (2012)

    Country comparison to the world: 6

Airports—With Paved Runways:

    Total: 159

    Over 3,047 m: 4

    2,438 to 3,047 m: 28

    1,524 to 2,437 m: 64

    914 to 1,523 m: 54

    Under 914 m: 9 (2012)

Airports—With Unpaved Runways:

    Total: 990

    Over 3,047 m: 1

    2,438 to 3,047 m: 1

    1,524 to 2,437 m: 45

    914 to 1,523 m: 499

    Under 914 m: 444 (2012)

Heliports:

    2 (2012)

Pipelines:

    Gas 29,401 km; liquid petroleum gas 41 km; oil 6,166 km; refined products 3,631 km (2010)

Railways:

    Total: 36,966 km

    Country comparison to the world: 8

Broad gauge: 26,475 km 1.676-m gauge (94 km electrified)

Standard gauge: 2,780 km 1.435-m gauge (42 km electrified)

Narrow gauge: 7,711 km 1.000-m gauge (2008)

Roadways:

Total: 231,374 km

Country comparison to the world: 21

Paved: 69,412 km (includes 734 km of expressways)

Unpaved: 161,962 km (2004)

Waterways:

11,000 km (2012)

Country comparison to the world: 12

Merchant Marine:

Total: 36

Country comparison to the world: 80

By type: bulk carrier 1, cargo 5, chemical tanker 6, container 1, passenger/cargo 1, petroleum tanker 18, refrigerated cargo 4

Foreign-owned: 14 (Brazil 1, Chile 6, Spain 3, Taiwan 2, UK 2)

Registered in other countries: 15 (Liberia 1, Panama 5, Paraguay 5, Uruguay 1, unknown 3) (2010)

Ports and Terminals:

Arroyo Seco, Bahia Blanca, Buenos Aires, La Plata, Punta Colorada, Rosario, San Lorenzo-San Martin, Ushuaia

Chapter 9: Military:

Military Branches:

Argentine Army (Ejercito Argentino), Navy of the Argentine Republic (Armada Republica; includes naval aviation and naval infantry), Argentine Air Force (Fuerza Aerea Argentina, FAA) (2011)

Military Service Age and Obligation:

18-24 years of age for voluntary military service (18-21 requires parental consent); no conscription (2001)

Manpower Available for Military Service:

Males age 16-49: 10,038,967

Females age 16-49: 9,959,134 (2010 est.)

Manpower Fit for Military Service:

Males age 16-49: 8,458,362

Females age 16-49: 8,414,460 (2010 est.)

Manpower Reaching Militarily Significant Age Annually:

Male: 339,503

Female: 323,170 (2010 est.)

Military Expenditures:

0.8% of GDP (2009)

Country comparison to the world: 146

Military—Note:

The Argentine military is a well-organized force constrained by the country's prolonged economic hardship; the country has recently experienced a strong recovery, and the military is implementing a modernization plan aimed at making the ground forces lighter and more responsive (2008)

Chapter 10: Transnational Issues

Disputes—International:

Argentina continues to assert its claims to the UK-administered Falkland Islands (Islas Malvinas), South Georgia, and the South Sandwich Islands in its constitution, forcibly occupying the Falklands in 1982, but in 1995 agreed to no longer seek settlement by force; UK continues to reject Argentine requests for sovereignty talks; territorial claim in Antarctica partially overlaps UK and Chilean claims; uncontested dispute between Brazil and Uruguay over Braziliera/Brasiliera Island in the Quarai/Cuareim River leaves the tripoint with Argentina in question; in 2010, the ICJ ruled in favor of Uruguay's operation of two paper mills on the Uruguay River, which forms the border with Argentina; the two countries formed a joint pollution monitoring regime; the joint boundary commission, established by Chile and Argentina in 2001 has yet to map and demarcate the delimited boundary in the inhospitable Andean Southern Ice Field (Campo de Hielo Sur); contraband smuggling, human trafficking, and illegal narcotic trafficking are problems in the porous areas of the border with Bolivia

Illicit Drugs:

A transshipment country for cocaine headed for Europe, heroin headed for the US, and ephedrine and pseudoephedrine headed for Mexico; some money-laundering activity, especially in the Tri-Border Area; law enforcement corruption; a source for precursor chemicals; increasing domestic consumption of drugs in urban centers, especially cocaine base and synthetic drugs (2008)

www.ingramcontent.com/pod-product-compliance
Lightning Source LLC
Chambersburg PA
CBHW070718180526
45167CB00004B/1526